HEAVENLY VERSE

Poetry for Inspiration

MIRANDA GUIRGUIS

WestBow Press books may be ordered through booksellers or by contacting:

WestBow Press
A Division of Thomas Nelson & Zondervan
1663 Liberty Drive
Bloomington, IN 47403
www.westbowpress.com
844-714-3454

ISBN: 979-8-3850-0870-4 (sc)
ISBN: 979-8-3850-0872-8 (hc)
ISBN: 979-8-3850-0871-1 (e)

Library of Congress Control Number: 2023918847

Print information available on the last page.

WestBow Press rev. date: 10/24/2023

WESTBOW
PRESS®
A DIVISION OF THOMAS NELSON
& ZONDERVAN

Contents

Acknowledgement
I'd like to thank Marcia and Hanja Krahn for the role they played in the editing process of my poems and for encouraging me with their prayers and kind words. You are a blessing.

Dedicated to:
My beautiful family: My two daughters, their spouses and my three grandchildren.
"As for me and my house, we will serve The Lord."
Joshua 24:15

HEAVENLY VERSE

GOD IS LOVE

Love knocks on the door, spreads wide a field of joy,
Content to hear our praise, reflects upon our gaze.
Bless The Lord, O my soul, and forget not in life's haze,
His warm embrace enfolds throughout each winter phase.

God is mercy and compassion. Great is The Holy One.
His loving touch restores to like upon a time was.
For harmony and cohesion, He cuts out harming lesions.
Master of His own scalpel, and jealously precise,
He will not leave you bleeding, but desperate for new heights.

When circumstances push to shove,
The workmanship of His Great Love
Causes captives to His Stronghold to return,
Releases prisoners of hope amid the burn.

All gains of this world, all its silver and gold,
Are no profit to the weary and desperate soul.
Like fish out of water floundering in the mud,
So we are bound to stray without this Greatest Love.
Behold. Draw near. Seek God's righteousness by faith.
All else are clanging cymbals, counterfeit's escapade.

HEAVENLY VERSE

From a tiny helpless seed to the outburst of a cry,
From the warm lull of her womb to the rush of light and sound.

Male and female He made them, God's one and only spectrum,
A world of snares awaits them, unless with His Spirit in tandem,
We raise them up to go His way of truth and life.
Created in God's own image, to His purpose our children tether,
Like arrows in the hand of a warrior, a quiver full to weather.

Not led with bit and bridle, not tossed nor flung by winds
Of confusion and division, injustice and derision,
A formula not in shortage bombards us every hour,
Our adversary ever seeks whom he may devour.

But a promise to Our Savior, before Him our knees we bend,
Our only weapon to overcome and the power of darkness rend.
Our sacrifice for a season yields a lifetime of God's delight,
Our children shall grow, reaping His endless streams of Light.

Teach them to taste and see, line upon line,
Precept upon precept, and a little at a time.
For to live by bread alone our children will not settle,
God's fragrance to the world, as sweet as honeysuckle.

So no matter what you see,
Declare your trust and cling.
This generation shall surely sing:
The Name of Jesus Christ as King.

EVRA KAADABER

Familiar Hebrew words of a determined endeavor,
For the hearer's delight, "Evra Kaadaber,"
Adopted by magic for spells and mystique,
Expresses its origin "I will create as I speak."

The power of a tongue capable of great starts,
Indeed, a little member, a spokesman of the heart.

From the fruit of one's lips, one shall be filled,
Words breathed out come alive, once instilled,
Cultivated in our thoughts, in our minds willed,
Unwittingly unlock gates to heaven or hell,
Capable to spring forth life or to death propel.

Words of life over circumstances, over what's been misconstrued,
Words of life over loved ones, which have no substitute,
Such fitly spoken words, upon Holy Spirit's nudge,
A powerful witness, which cannot be judged.
Hence, The God who gives wings to the prayers of His own,
Hears from Heaven above, purposing what has been sown.

HEAVENLY VERSE

"God is good," exulted the preacher.
"All the time," confirmed the saints,
Poised to declare with rejoicing,
"The Lord our Inheritance, our only boasting."

Dry bones and barren lives, in the blink of an eye,
The Potter's new creation, for God can't tell a lie.
Prodigals run home, His mercies on display,
The unfamiliar springs up, old things have passed away.

Power to run and not grow weary, power to walk and not faint.

How great is The Holy One? How magnificent is His work?
The same yesterday, today, always, and forever,
All-powerful, ever-present, all-knowing, ever-loving!

New eyes open to see His splendor and might,
His effortless symphony, ears' marvel of delight,
For which we confess in unison, upon cue,
"Maker of all things Wonderfully New,
By Your amazing grace, death forever withdrew.
Indeed, God, You are good!
All the time, You are good!"

HEAVENLY VERSE

Out of Egypt You called me forth,
But to Baal I have sacrificed.
Drawn away by my own desires,
Enveloped by the snares, mummified.
Dug holes so deep in the games of ties,
Put trust in the voices of many lies.

All smoke and mirrors derail my trek,
My own competition stares me back.
Misled by the mirage of emotional bubble,
In the waterless pit, You restore to me double.

Teach me to walk again, O Lord, take me gently by the hand.
Heal my brokenness, O Lord, cement my feet upon Your land.

You alone are God, and man is not.
You peel back the mask and judge the heart.
When outward appearances advertise,
Your unveiling reveals their bogus disguise.

A silhouette of radiance, the character of a good man,
Brightly shines against the halo of the Sun,
Obediently considers the plank in his own eye,
This lamp of the body, its importance realized.
A reflection of the Divine residing inside,
The hope of glory in the darkest of times.

HEAVENLY VERSE

Maker of Heaven and Earth, the Living God Almighty,
The Everlasting Father, Prince of Peace,
Creation's Designer, The Lord our Zeal.
How could fools shore up, in blind stubbornness, such resistance?
How could hearts harden, reject His undeniable existence?

Ideas of Who God is, obstinately preconceived,
In their human minds unnaturally perceived.
Distortedly view Him in a ridiculous chase,
Wrongly appeal their insignificant case.

God's picture marred amid the whirl
Of many dark clouds over a fallen world,
Falsified in cynicism to the very end,
Walled in many wars of discontent.

Surrounded by His loveliness, I stand amazed
In His abundant Mercy, Kindness, and Grace.
Jesus, Our High Priest, Heaven's Dear,
His glorious light dispels every fear,
Confounds the wise, makes all clear,
Conveys that I am what I am today,
Because The Great I AM is the Who I AM, always!

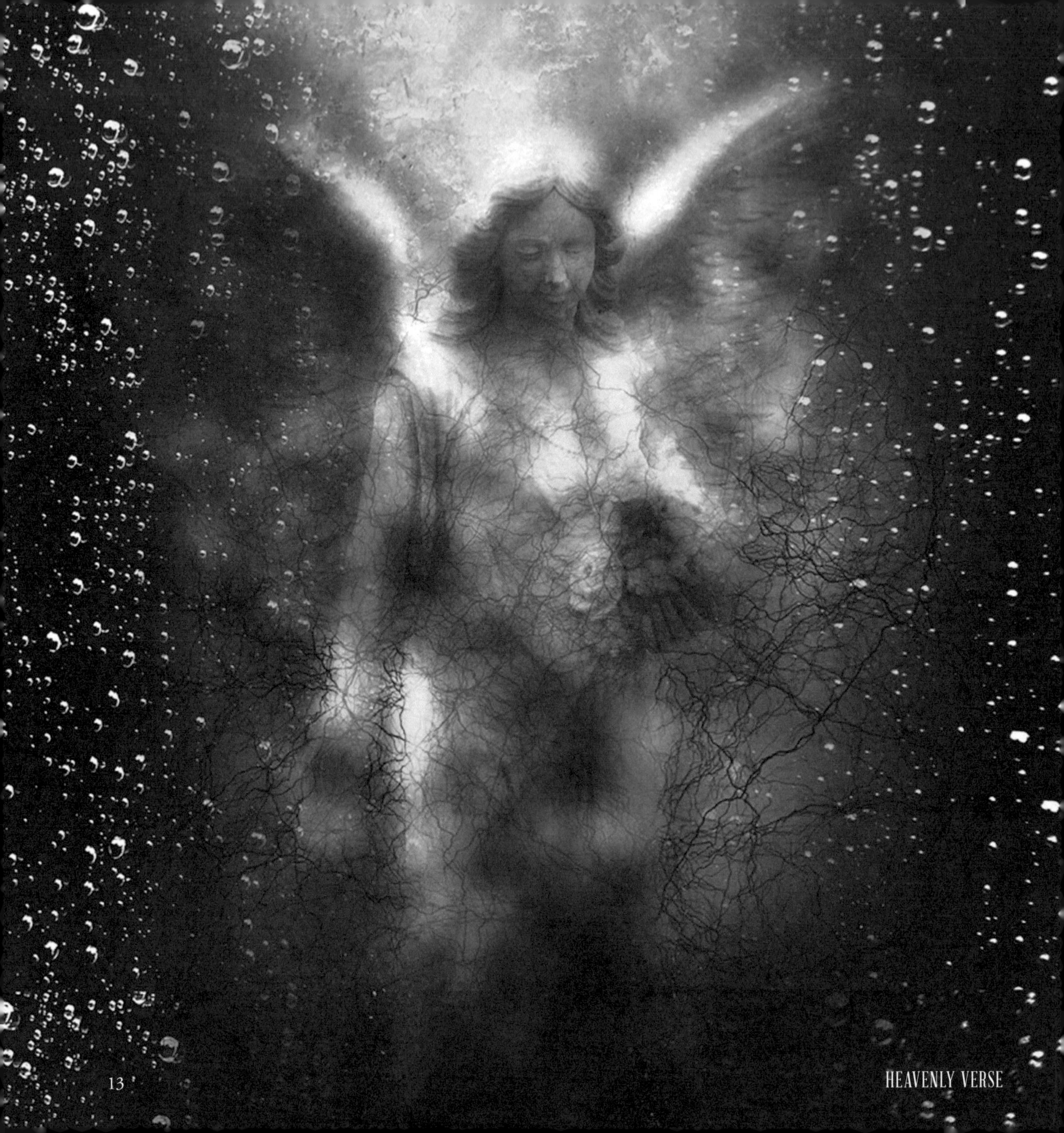

"I'm giving for you a word," declared the prophet.
"Its meaning a treasure I must deposit.
I saw shimmering light all around you,
A majestic angel stood tall before you.
Spread his wings wide, poised to guard you.
His voice permeated the atmosphere,
Dispelled with these words your mounting fear:

    'The Lord is zealous for your intentions.
    Apply your heart to these instructions.
    Obey The Word, increase your knowledge.
    In all your ways, The Lord acknowledge.
    Meekness is not weakness, but power under control.
    Forgiveness is not yielding, but ransom for your soul.
    Give Him all your heart, look to Him each day.
    Look up for redemption far beyond the Milky Way.
    From the bite of a serpent and the sting of a viper,
    He shall be your Protector, your Shield and Defender.
    Highly esteemed worldly gains and desires,
    God does not hold dear, nor does He require.
    For you, Beloved, He shall set apart,
    His favor is upon you, His Spirit He imparts.
    No longer held down but made free indeed.
    Spread your wings to fly. Release The Powerful Seed!'

Then the angel shined his light pointing out the way.
Assigned to you a new name, in God's grace, that day."

HEAVENLY VERSE

Parallel our DNA, uniquely bestowed,
The very breath of God in our being flows.
    God-predestined, not self-made.
    God-dependent, not self-ruled.
For those who believe, no explanation needed.
For those who doubt, no explanation possible.

When forsaken, abandoned, and left to roam,
A squandered sojourner without a home,
The Father, in mercy, beckons with favor,
Welcomes all as His children, never as strangers.

For whosoever believes is a child of The King.
Created in God's own image to do great things.
Dreams conceived, yet to decode, are dreams in the making,
Despite how things appear, we trust and keep waiting.
To know we are His Seed, according to the promise,
To know our true value, our greatest source of solace,
No matter our status, or circle of influence,
No matter our color, ethnicity, or affluence,
All in the family, by His Love and Grace,
All in the family, a heritage to embrace.

O Hail, King Jesus! He triumphed over death.
O Hail, Redeemer! He paid our eternal debt.

At the right hand of God, His Throne was held reserved,
While separated From His Father for our rebirth.
By His shed blood, death He overcame,
Subjugated all rivals by the power in His Name.
By His Broken body, He absolved our scorn.
Sacrificially our shame on Calvary was borne.

When His final breath on the cross He took,
The earth grieved in sorrow and violently shook.
From top to bottom, the veil in two was torn.
By conquering death, His righteousness we adorn.

Fear and confusion gripped those He faithfully led,
With doubts they scattered just like He said.
But on the third day, He arose from the dead.
His body in the grave no longer lays,
He fulfilled our destiny, paved for us the way.
O Hail, King Jesus!

His trumpeted entrance, in a moment will appear.
Our Heavenly Home has forever been sealed.
Face-to-face with His glory, for now we can only yearn,
Until the Great Day of His triumphant return!
O Hail, King Jesus!

MIRANDA GUIRGUIS

HEAVENLY VERSE

With God all things are possible,
Without Him, we build in vain.
Our Rock sufficiently able,
Guards against offenses' gain.

His Grace through Faith abounds,
Heavenly homes await the Found.
Old things diligently renewed,
A new life in Christ endued.

At The Cross our future built,
Set free from every guilt.
Brought out from darkness to light,
Made perfect in His Holy Sight.

Our tomorrow is the hope of yesterday,
Redemption at our beckoning call,
His lasting rich abundance,
Our adoption secured and installed.

To The One Who Was and Is, and Is to come, we praise.
Worthy King of kings, to Our Lord we give all our days.

21

In a land of carved images, The Holy One stands tall,
Leads me through unruly waters, picks me up when I fall.
Makes Rivers in the desert, in wilderness charts routes,
The God of salvation, He shut the lions' mouth.

He takes in the rejected and anyone forsaken.
The mistreated and abused, He has not forgotten.
He cares for the destitute and considers the outcasts.
The Lord is our Lawgiver, His judgement is the last.
He advocates for the accused and the unjustly blamed,
In Him there is no partiality, He loves us all the same.

Doubts and fears, burdens, and worries, the hurt and the pain,
Cast them all upon The One whose cross replaced our shame.
His finished work is our portion, it stands the test of time,
This battle already has been won, no more hills to climb.

One thing Our God desires, a humble, sincere heart,
To bring good news to the poor, His Joy to impart.
Our weapons of renewal, by His Spirit not by might,
To build a house of faith, to be The Lord's delight.
So, we lay down our struggles, we lighten up our load,
Put on His whole armor and stand against our foes.

HEAVENLY VERSE

My Helper

The Lord, who made Heaven and Earth, watches over me since birth,
With gladness makes me whole; He shall preserve my soul.

My eyes are upon You, O Lord, in You I shall take refuge.
When floods of unrest arise, You shelter me from deluge.
When snares laid up for sport, to You I run to resort.
You are my only source, my endurance to stay the course.

In my distress You hear me, O LORD, my Peace and Strength.
Your pillar of light before me, my focus in battle's length.
Many treasures within Your courts, freely given to all who wait,
For Your arm is not too short, and Your timing is never late.

In fervor without ceasing, by day and evening glow,
On mountaintop events, or in valley windings low,
My mouth with shouts will praise You, from my spirit freely flow.

The LORD is my Keeper, my Shield, and my Buckler,
My Hope, my Deliverer, The LORD my Provider.
My God is in the waiting, He shall not leave me wanting.
My Helper, my Friend, my Forever abiding.

HEAVENLY VERSE

Let not the power of wisdom become our boast.
Let not the power of riches become our cost.
Let not the power of fame become our quest.
Let him who exalts glory in Jesus Christ.

In this disorderly world with faction's upheaval,
Hostilities blaze between the good and the evil.
Against such we do not wrestle, in our own strength,
Being watchful, steadfast, assured by faith
That we stand undefeated, and forever secure,
For God's written Word quickens us to mature.

Therefore, we walk circumspectly, not as fools but as wise,
Satiated with Christ's Spirit, to redeem the time.
With clean hands and minds, pure thoughts, and hearts,
Flee temptations, turn around, determine to depart!
Good riddance shame and doubt! Good riddance daily scum!
Good riddance to the notion we can never overcome!
God's fullness of joy promises to undergird,
For our power is in the washing of The Word.

HEAVENLY VERSE

Not an ordinary fish, an example uncommon,
A life cycle proved worthy of reexamining.
Its journey upstream, arduously demanding,
A test of impressive will, endurance, and stamina,
Depositing multitudes of tiny salmon ova.

Male and female barge into a river hollow,
In a simultaneous dance, where water is shallow.
Spawn in the same place, once upon a time hatched,
Release their own kind, in gravel beds to latch,
Then swim away trusting, their vulnerable younglings,
To adulthood thrust, amid nature's bustling.
A short life, nonetheless, with one goal in mind,
To lay it all down for offspring left behind.

Go to the salmon, you of little faith,
                    consider its ways, be wise!
Having no captain, no overseer,
                    against all chance, the odds defy.

How long will your fears host you in prison?
How long will the doubts drown your God-given vision?

Worth all cost to the point of dying,
                    Hail all efforts in pursuit of trying.
One's life for another, a love beyond measure,
                    In due season, cycles life-giving treasure.

At the break of dawn, as early clouds disappear,
In anticipation I wait for My Lord to draw near.
Despite all the noise, constant daily intrusions,
He establishes my steps amid all the confusion.
His voice in the silence undoubtedly clear,
As the coo of a dove, His song I hear.

Prone to doubt, quick to wander,
Yet He brings me out to ponder.
In the stillness cacophony dims,
Contemplating things of Him.
Things that are noble, just, and pure,
Lovely things, and of good report,
Things of virtue, my heart to allure.
                              Selah

A world of choices, and voices so loud,
But in the quietness, His alone abounds:
    "My Beloved, pause and listen,
    Guard your heart and mind from glisten,
    Tend them as a garden, flee the clamor,
    Find My peace, abandon glamour."
                              Selah

Your Goodness, O Lord, in meditation I shall seek.
Of Your Righteousness, my tongue shall always speak.
Within Your Light, Truth be told,
How deficient am I on my own.
Distractions and worries, such breathless haste,
Can't add a cubit — such mindless waste!

HEAVENLY VERSE

A declaration by many, again and again,
God's not bound by time, nor subject to space.
Hard to understand, or rightfully explain,
Upon His beloved children, He has bestowed this grace:

There is more to the space we survey and occupy.
There is more to this moment in time far beyond,
More to physical factors, not bound by what is seen,
More to temporal successions, living outside what is esteemed.

Each word fitly spoken, each impulsive act of kindness,
Every prayer, every praise, every hope for goodness,
He takes out of our own hands, into His when we ask,
With wings released to fly, limitlessly into the by-and-by,
Accomplishes the impossible, greater things unimaginable.

We are living stones in God's infinite plan,
A lasting house being built with His own Hands.
Praise be to God! Praise to The Holy One Divine!
His limitlessness is ours, by His own design.

HEAVENLY VERSE

Let us draw near with a true heart
        in full assurance of faith,
Our great High Priest of Heaven
        pulled back the dividing lace.

In the face of the one seductive,
        we trust The Spirit of Truth,
Leaning on Our Lord's directives
        to guard the paths of cues.

When an offering to spare is hard,
        with obedience little is much.
Freedom from money's clutch
        springs from The Father's touch.

Beneath long-awaited dew,
        when the ground is desert-dry,
Love wells up just in time,
        captures honor above the lie.

The diligent soul made rich,
        when surrounding affairs unhinge,
Holds loosely earthly possessions,
        to incorruptible riches clings.

A house of lasting treasures
        pursues generations to come,
With a wealth of righteousness and wisdom,
        to the beat of their hearts' drum,
Spiritual millionaires in the making
        remain in The Holy One.

HEAVENLY VERSE

Casting down imaginations,
        Never alone, never forsaken,
By abiding in the Most High,
        In His secret place I hide.

Dare to imagine, dare to dream,
        Beneath shadows of pollution.
Clouds of self-will dissipate
        In Jesus's act of substitution.

A God-given freedom, bright and swift.
        A spiritual awakening, a paradigm shift.

Co-heirs with Christ, according to the promise,
        Pursue the voice of peace and solace.
Undeniably peculiar,
        Choose the path that's least familiar.

This life is not my own,
        But Jesus Christ's, my Cornerstone.

WAVE YOUR SWORD!

Sometimes cuts and sometimes cures,
        Sometimes hurts and sometimes heals,
This double-edged Sword slices and saves,
        Sometimes exposes, God's heart reveals.
Covers from harm, our soul conceals,
        Warns us from temptation to steer.
Shines a light on the firm foundation,
        The Written Word, the Rock of salvation.

When fiery trials appear face-to-face,
        Count it all joy for your testing of faith.
Wave the Sword of Holy Truth,
        The matchless weapon of no substitute.
Mustering courage, in such to stand strong,
        Rejecting the intertwining of worldly wrongs.

Our lineage of sustenance,
        Within His Providence,
Our fight for Heaven's dominance,
        Our gaining with confidence.

HEAVENLY VERSE

O Church, Rise Up!

Our time is now to speak, whether in season or out.
Justice we must seek, break the chains of doubt.
Give hope to the hopeless, defend the fatherless,
Draw men unto Christ and plead for the widow.
O Church, Rise up!

For sin The Law was born, but in His Favor Mercy is found,
Our redemption He adorned, by faith His Love to abound.
All you downcast believe, to the Joy of The Lord cleave.
Delight in planting good, in due season we shall reap.
We grow not weary nor fret, it only causes much regret.
Powerfully together let us band, a house divided cannot stand.
O Church, Rise up!

A world of security in temporal and selfish pleasures,
Can only boast labor and sorrow beyond measure.
O Church, Rise up!

Count the cost, consider Him worthy,
Unparalleled is His Crown of Glory.
Be diligent and without shame,
Magnify The Master's Name.
In His Courts our spirit shall dwell,
Cast His Seed boldly to tell,
Watch Him break the gates of hell,
Doors of bronze and bars of iron,
Patiently wait for our promised Zion.

O Church, rise up and speak,
Rightly discerning the Word of Truth.
Christ for all, in Him our being,
To die is gain, His ways must choose,
Lift Him up, give Him all Glory,
Shout to the world Our Grace-filled story!

Miranda Guirguis

Poem References

O Church Rise up
Isaiah 1:17
Philippians 1:21-26
Isaiah 45:2
Salmon
Proverbs 6:6-8
Selah
Philippians 4:8
Space and Time
1 Peter 2:5
Spiritual Millionaires
Proverbs 13:4
Colossians 3:2
True surrender
Psalm 91:1
Wave your Sword!
James 1:2-3
Power Washing
Ephesians 5:15-18
2 Timothy 2:22

My Helper
Psalm 121
Psalm 20:7
It is Finished
Psalm 51:17
Parents' Declaration
Psalm 127:4-5
God is Love
Zechariah 9:12
I Corinthians 13:1-2
Wonderfully New
2 Corinthians 5:17
Isaiah 40:31
Mirror, Mirror on The Wall
Matthew 7:3-5
Evra Kadaaber
James 3:5
Tomorrow Starts Yesterday
Psalm 127:4-5

Printed in the United States
by Baker & Taylor Publisher Services